FlyHigh
Pupil's Book
2

Jeanne Perrett   Charlotte Covill

T0385907

FlyHigh 2 — Contents

 **Alphabet**

 **A a** /eɪ/

 B b /biː/

 **C c** /siː/

 D d /diː/

1 **Listen and say.**

Hello, I'm Chatter. What's your name?
Let's learn: a, b, c, d.

2 **Listen and write.**

apple /æ/

a   a   a

A   A   A

bear /b/

b   b   b

B   B   B

cat /k/

c   c   c

C   C   C

dog /d/

d   d   d

D   D   D

Find and match.

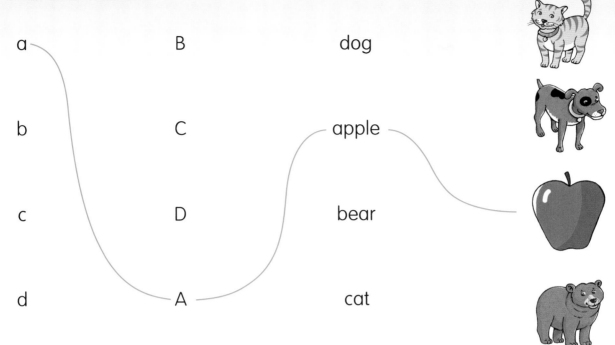

a   B   dog

b   C   apple

c   D   bear

d   A   cat

 Listen and circle.

1   

2

3

4

 Complete and sing.

a b .... d

Alphabet

 **E e**
/iː/

 F f
/ef/

 G g
/dʒiː/

 H h
/eɪtʃ/

1 **Listen and say.**

> Hello, I'm Tag. How are you?
> Let's learn: e, f, g, h.

2 **Listen and write.**

/e/

elephant

 e e e
E E E

/f/

flower

 f f f
F F F

/g/

goat

 g g g
G G G

/h/

hippo

h h h
H H H

3 Match and write.

e   f   g   h

......ippo   e lephant   ......lower   ......oat

4 Find and circle.

a	D	A	C	B
b	B	D	A	C
c	A	B	C	D
d	B	C	A	D

5 Listen and circle.

1

2

3

4

6 Complete and sing.

a ...... c ...... e f ...... h

Alphabet

 **I i**
/aɪ/

 J j
/dʒeɪ/

 K k
/keɪ/

 L l
/el/

1 **Listen and say.**

Hello, I'm Karla. What's your name?
Let's learn: i, j, k, l.

2 **Listen and write.**

 /ɪ/
insect

 /dʒ/
jelly

 /k/
kangaroo

 /l/
lion

3 **Find and match.**

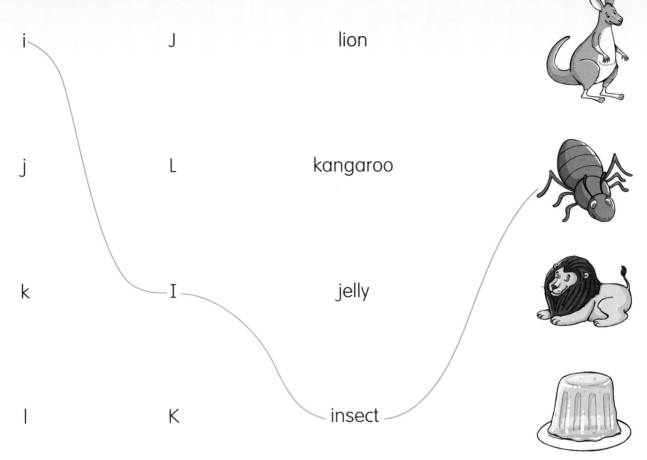

i   J   lion

j   L   kangaroo

k   I   jelly

l   K   insect

4 **Match.**

b   c   i   f   g   k

G   K   B   C   F   I

5 **Complete and sing.** 🖸

...... b c ...... e ...... g ...... i j l

Alphabet

M m /em/

N n /en/

O o /əʊ/

P p /piː/

(1) **Listen and say.**

Hi, I'm Patty. How are you?
Let's learn: m, n, o, p.

(2) **Listen and write.**

monkey /m/   m m m   M M M M

nest /n/   n n n   N N N

octopus /ɒ/   o o o   O O O

penguin /p/   p p p   P P P

3 **Match and write.**

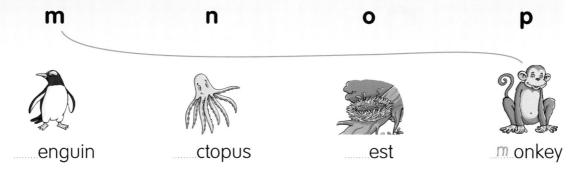

m   **n**   **o**   **p**

.......enguin   ....ctopus   ....est   m...onkey

4 **Find and circle.**

g	Ⓖ	E	C	D
j	H	G	I	J
m	N	B	M	P
o	F	O	L	D

5 **Listen and circle.**

1

2

3

4

6 **Complete and sing.**

a .... d .... f g .... i .... k l .... n .... p

**Alphabet**

**Q q**
/kjuː/

R r
/aː/

**S s**
/es/

T t
/tiː/

1 **Listen and say.**

Hi, I'm Trumpet. What's your name?
Let's learn: q, r, s, t.

2 **Listen and write.**

queen
/kw/

rabbit
/r/

snake
/s/

tiger
/t/

3 Find and match.

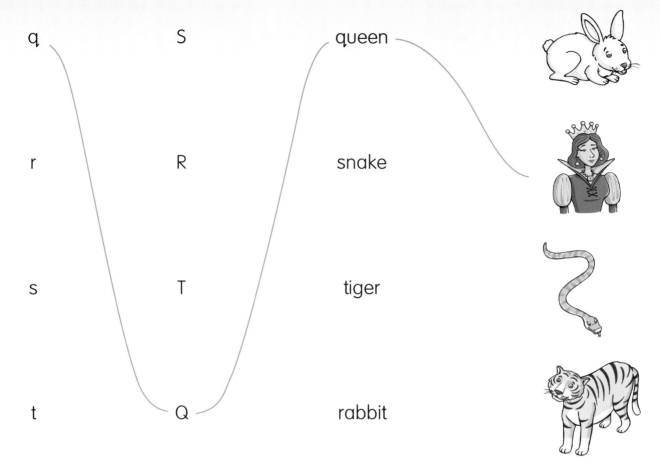

q   S   queen

r   R   snake

s   T   tiger

t   Q   rabbit

4 Match.

a   e   h   l   m   n   q   r

H   A   L   R   N   E   M   Q

5 Complete and sing.

a b ...... d ...... g ...... i j .... m ...... o ...... q ...... s ......

Alphabet

U u /juː/

W w /ˈdʌbəljuː/

V v /viː/

1 Listen and say.

Hi. I'm Sally. How are you?
Let's learn: u, v, w.

2 Listen and write.

umbrella   /ʌ/

 U U U U
U U U U

vulture   /v/

 V V V
V V V V

whale   /w/

W W W
W W W

3 Match and write.

U   V   W

.......hale   u mbrella   ....ulture

4 Listen and circle.

1

2

3

4

5 Complete and sing.

a .... c .... f .... h i .... l .... n .... p .... r .... u v ....

Alphabet

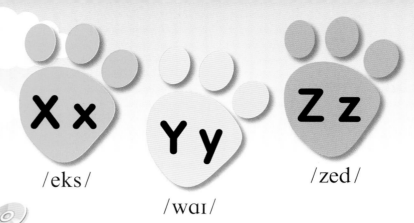

X x /eks/

Y y /waɪ/

Z z /zed/

1 **Listen and write.**

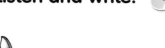

fo**x** /ks/

X X X
X X X

yo-yo /j/

y y y
Y Y Y

zebra /z/

Z Z Z
Z Z Z

2 **Find and match.**

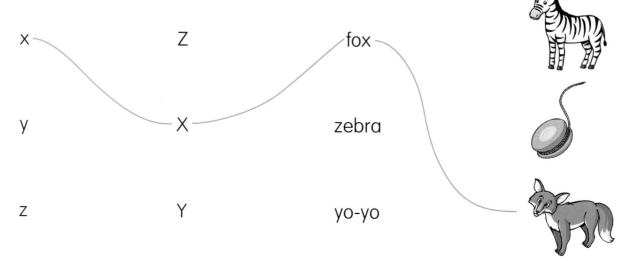

X   Z   fox

y   X   zebra

z   Y   yo-yo

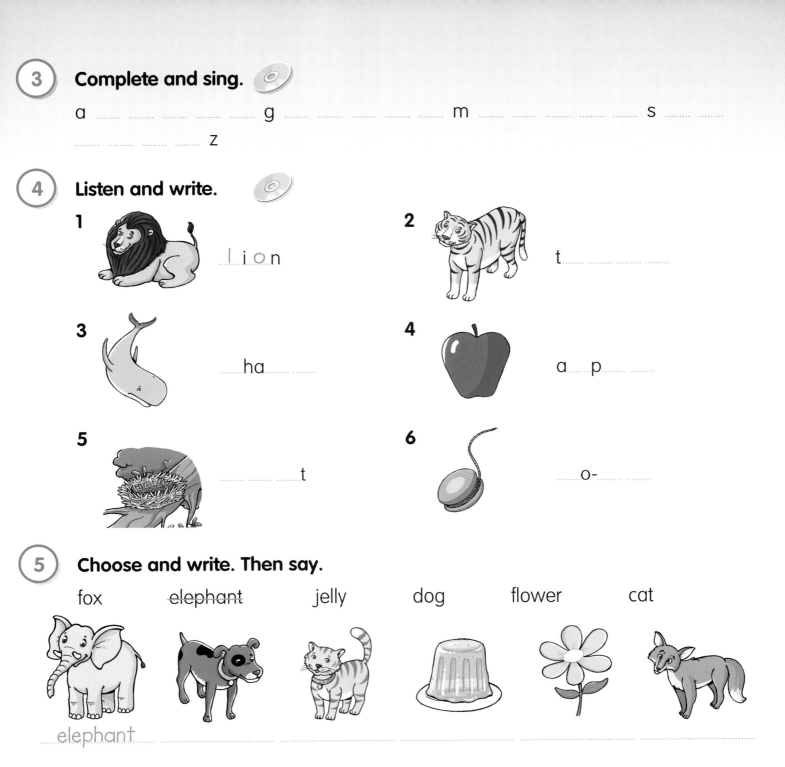

3 Complete and sing.

a .... g .... m .... s ....

.... z

4 Listen and write.

1 l i o n

2 t ....

3 ....ha..........

4 a.......... p..........

5 .... t

6 ....o-..........

5 Choose and write. Then say.

fox   ~~elephant~~   jelly   dog   flower   cat

elephant ....

6 Play the game.

How do you spell 'elephant'?

e...l...e...p...h...a...n...t

Colours

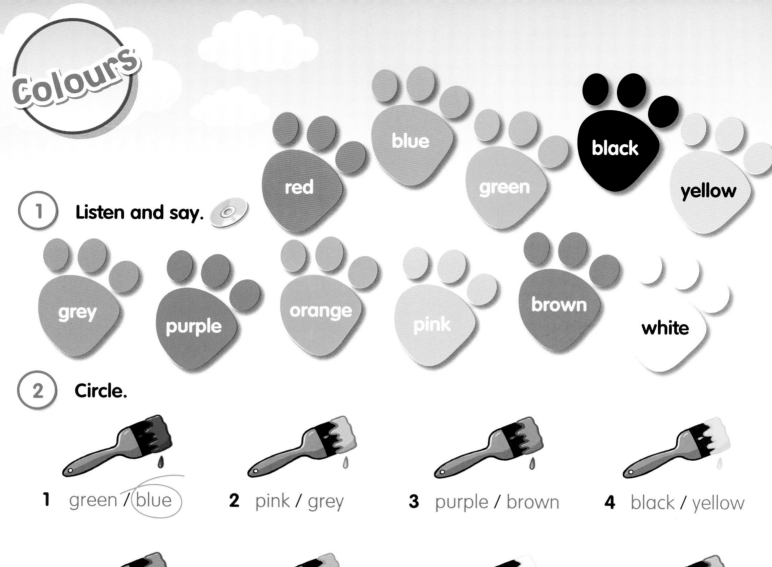

① **Listen and say.**

red · blue · green · black · yellow
grey · purple · orange · pink · brown · white

② **Circle.**

1 green / blue

2 pink / grey

3 purple / brown

4 black / yellow

5 white / red

6 orange / blue

7 yellow / white

8 black / grey

③ **Sing along with the FlyHigh band!** ♫

The colours song
Red and white and pink,
Yellow, green and blue.
Grey and black and brown,
Orange and purple too.
Colours in the zoo for you!

OUR ZOO

4 Colour.

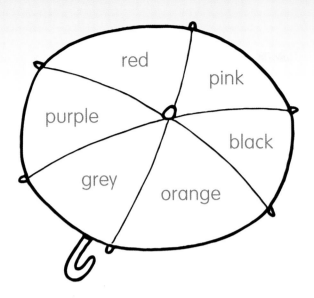
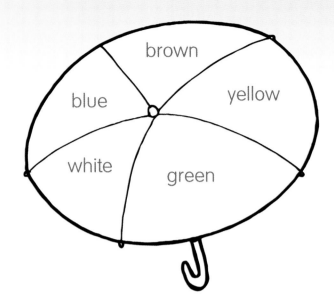

5 Write. Then play the game.

.......red....... ....

....

orange

fox

....

1 Listen and say.

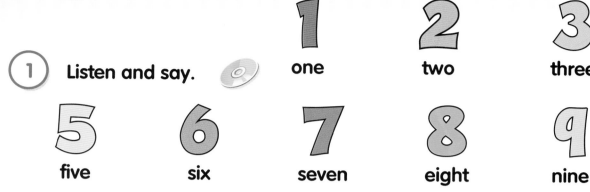

1 one
2 two
3 three
4 four

5 five
6 six
7 seven
8 eight
9 nine
10 ten

2 Listen and circle.

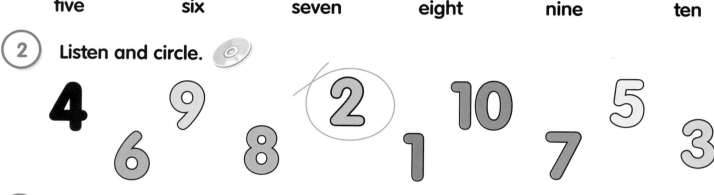

4 9 2 10 5

6 8 1 7 3

3 Write and match.

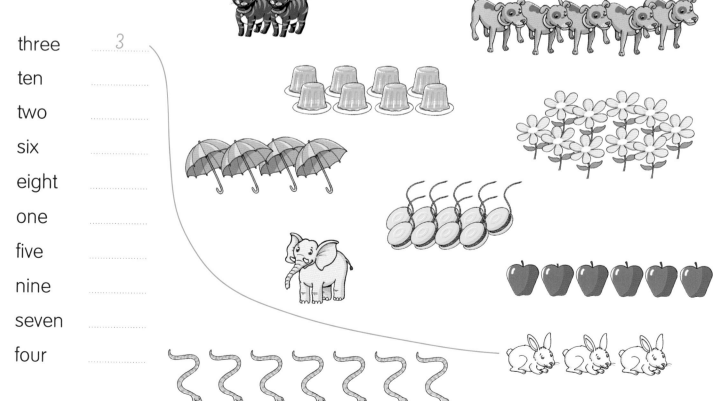

three   3

ten

two

six

eight

one

five

nine

seven

four

4 Sing along with the **FlyHigh** band! 🎵

The numbers song

One, two, three, four, five,
Six, seven, eight, nine, ten.
One, two, three, four, five,
Six, seven, eight, nine, ten.

Then colour by number.

5 Play the game.

3

7

Bingo!

school bag pencil pen rubber book

It's a school!

1 **Circle.**

1 It's a book. yes / no **2** It's a pencil. yes / no

3 It's a rubber. yes / no **4** It's a bag. yes / no

Learn with Tag

a b c d e f g h i j k l m
n o p q r s t u v w x y z

What's this? It's a book. It's an apple.

2. Write a or an.

1. It's ___a___ bag.
2. It's _____ umbrella.
3. It's _____ elephant.

4. It's _____ pencil.
5. It's _____ monkey.
6. It's _____ octopus.

3. Listen and stick. Then circle.

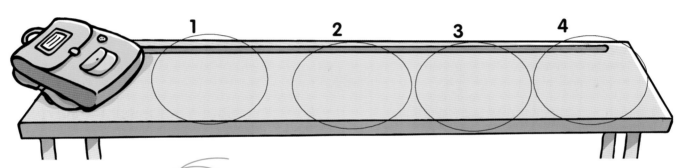

1. What's this? It's a (book)/ pen.
2. What's this? It's a pencil / rubber.

3. What's this? It's a rubber / pen.
4. What's this? It's a pencil / book.

4. Sing along with the FlyHigh band! 🎵

What's this?
What's this? What is this?
What's this in my bag?
What's this? What is this?
What's this in my bag?
What's this? It's a pencil.
A pencil and a pen.
A pencil, a rubber, a book and a pen.
A pencil, a rubber, a book and a pen.

 spell   chair   write   board   be quiet

Spell octopus.

① What's this?

It's a chair.

Yes. Spell 'chair', please.

c...h...a...i...r

② Very good, Patty! Tag, write on the board, please. Write 'cat'.

③ Karla, what's this?

It's an octopus. The octopus is purple.

I'm an octopus.

④ Be quiet, please, Chatter.

Spell 'octopus'!

o...k...a...

No. It's o...c...t...

1   **Match.**

1 What's

2 Spell

3 Write on

4 Be

a the board, please.

b 'chair', please.

c quiet, please.

d this?

It's an octopus. The octopus is purple.
It's a cat. The cat is black.

2 **Write** a, an **or** The.

1 It's ...an... umbrella. ...The... umbrella is red.
2 It's .... pencil. .... pencil is yellow.
3 It's .... board. .... board is white.
4 It's .... chair. .... chair is brown.
5 It's .... insect. .... insect is green.

3 **Play the game.**

4 **Write with Karla.**

3

 car ball doll stickers crayon  card

Cars and balls!

1

What are they, Karla?

They're balls!

Red, yellow, green and blue balls!

2

What are they?

They're cars. Orange cars.

Trumpet! Come here, please.

3

What are they, Sally?

They're dolls and stickers and crayons.

Thank you, Sally.

4

Look! A card!

Happy Birthday Sally

1 **Write** yes **or** no.

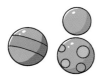         

1 green balls   **2** black cars   **3** yellow stickers   **4** blue crayons

    yes

Learn with Tag

What are they?

They're balls. One ball, two balls, three balls.

2 **Circle.**

1 a ball / balls   **2** a doll / dolls   **3** a car / cars   **4** a crayon / crayons

3 **Ask and answer.**

Number five. What are they?

They're crayons.

 1
 2
 3
 4
 5
 6
 7
 8
 9

4 **Sing along with the FlyHigh band!**

Cars and dolls

Orange cars and
Yellow cars.
Cars for me and you!
One, two, three, four.
Lots of cars.
Cars for me and you.

Purple dolls and
Big, pink dolls.
Dolls for me and you!
One, two, three, four.
Lots of dolls.
Dolls for me and you.

4

robot

birthday

cake

present

watch

That's a robot!

1 It's my birthday. This is my cake.

Happy Birthday, Sally!

Thank you.

2 What are they?

They're your presents.

3 This is a watch and that is a pen.

Thank you. They're lovely presents.

4 That's a robot.

Thank you, Tag!

1 **Match.**

1  They're your presents. **a**

2   That's a robot. **b**

3   This is my cake. **c**

Learn with Tag

This is a watch.

That is a robot.

2 Circle and write.

1 (This) / That is a ....cake........ .

2 This / That is a ....

3 This / That is a ....

4 This / That is a ....

3 Listen and stick.

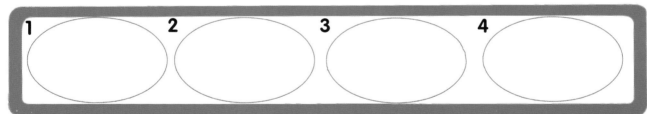

| 1 | 2 | 3 | 4 |

4 Play the game.

Guess!

No! This is a yellow pencil and that is a red pencil.

This is a red pencil and that is a yellow pencil.

Sally's Story

The frogs!

 frog
 teacher
 close
 door

1 What's this? It's a school. Look! A teacher.

2 Look! What are they? Frogs!

3 Lots of frogs! Close the door!

4 Close the window!

---

1 **Count and write.**

1 ......four frogs...... **2** .... **3** ....

window

stand up

open

sit down

5

What's this?

It's a pencil.

What's that?

It's a board.

6

Stand up!

7

Open the door!

Open the window!

Goodbye!

8

Sit down, please.

Goodbye, frogs!

2 **Write with Karla.**

My name is Karla.
This is my bag.
The bag is red.
The pencil is yellow.
The rubber is blue.

My name is ....
This ....
The ....
....
....

1 Write.

1 What's this? It's _____a doll_____ .

2 What's this? It's _____ .

3 What's this? It's _____ .

4 What's this? It's _____ .

2 Listen and stick. Then write yes or no.

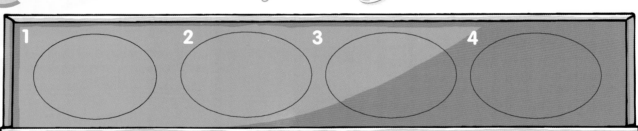

1 The crayon is yellow. _____no_____

2 The book is pink. _____

3 The pen is red. _____

4 The rubber is green. _____

3 Match.

1 Open the door. _____d_____

2 Close the window. _____

3 Stand up. _____

4 Sit down. _____

5 Write on the board. _____

6 Be quiet. _____

a

b

c

d

e

f

4 Write.

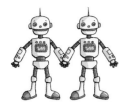

1 robots   **2** ....   **3** ....   **4** ....

5 Circle and write.

1 This is / (That is) a robot .   **2** This is / That is ....

3 This is / That is ....   **4** This is / That is ....

My Project What's in your school bag? Write a list. Draw.

- a pen
- two yellow crayons
- a rubber
- four books
- three pencils

Now go to
My Picture Dictionary

5

 family   mum   dad   brother   sister

sunny

She's pretty.

(1) **Match.**

1 mum   **2** dad   **3** sister   **4** brother

a   **b**   **c**    **d**

Learn with Tag

I am Tag. I'm a tiger.

I am → I'm	He is → He's
You are → You're	She is → She's
	It is → It's

2 **Write** am, are **or** is.

1 I ...am... Trumpet.

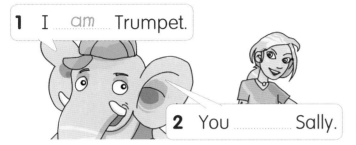

2 You .... Sally.

3 He .... Chatter.

4 She .... Patty.

3 **Listen and stick. Then circle.**

1 She's my mum /(sister.)
2 He's my dad / brother.

3 He's my dad / brother.
4 She's my mum / sister.

4 **Sing along with** the **FlyHigh** band! 🎵

My family

Clap and dance and sing with me.
Sing about my family.
He's my brother.
She's my sister.
He's my dad
And she's my mum.
Clap and dance and sing with me.
Sing about my family.

6

 grandpa   baby   boy   girl   grandma   friend

Is he your grandpa?

1) **Match.**

1 He's my grandpa.   **2** She's my sister.   **3** He's my friend.   **4** She's my grandma.

a   **b**   **c**    **d**

Are you a girl?

Yes, I am.

Learn with Tag

Am I ...?	Yes, you are./No, you aren't.
Are you ...?	Yes, I am./No, I'm not.
Is he ...?	Yes, he is./No, he isn't.
Is she ...?	Yes, she is./No, she isn't.
Is it ...?	Yes, it is./No, it isn't.

(2) Ask and answer.

a teacher   a boy   a girl   a baby

Are you a teacher?

No, I'm not.

(3) Write Yes, he is/Yes, she is **or** No, he isn't/No, she isn't.

1   Is she a penguin?
   ....Yes, she is.........

2   Is he a tiger?
   ....

3   Is he an elephant?
   ....

4   Is she a monkey?
   ....

(4) Write with Karla.

My name's Karla. I'm a girl. I'm eight.

My name's ....
I'm ....
I'm ....

cowboy box clothes spy  dancer

We're cowboys.

1 Wow! Look!

Let's go.

2 Open the box. What are they?

They're clothes.

3 Wow, Patty! You're a spy.

You're a dancer.

4 We're cowboys!

Be careful, Chatter.

Sorry, Trumpet.

1 **Match.**

1 It's a box.   **2** She's a dancer.   **3** He's a cowboy.   **4** She's a spy.

a    **b**    **c**   **d**

Learn with Tag

We're cowboys.

We are cowboys. → We're cowboys.
You are dancers. → You're dancers.
They are friends. → They're friends.

2 **Write** We are, You are **or** They are.

1 ...... We are ...... monkeys.

2 .... kangaroos.

3 .... penguins.

3 **Read and cross (X).**

1 You're dancers.

a  b

2 We're cowboys.

a b

3 They're girls.

a  b

4 They're clothes.

a  b

4 **Sing along with the FlyHigh band!** ♫

We're happy today.

Stand up and say
We're happy today,
Happy today, happy today.

Sit down and say
We're happy today,
Happy today, happy today.

Clap hands and say
We're happy today,
Happy today,
happy today.

 pirate
 clown
 king
 crown

8

Are we pirates? ♫

1
Are we pirates?
Are we clowns?
Are we kings
With golden crowns?
Look and see,
Look and see,
What are we?
Look and see,
Look and see,
What are we?

2
Are we dancers?
Are we clowns?
Are we queens
With golden crowns?
Look and see,
Look and see,
What are we?
Look and see,
Look and see,
What are we?

3
Are they dancers?
Are they clowns?
Are they queens
With golden crowns?
Look and say,
Look and say,
What are they?
Look and say,
Look and say,
What are they?

4
Are they pirates?
Are they clowns?
Are they kings
With golden crowns?
Look and say,
Look and say,
What are they?
Look and say,
Look and say,
What are they?

1 **Circle.**

1 Tag is a cowboy / pirate.
2 Chatter isn't a pirate / king.
3 Karla is a spy / clown.
4 Patty isn't a clown / queen.

Are we clowns?

No, we aren't.

Learn with Tag

Are we queens? Yes, you are./No, you aren't.
Are you clowns? Yes, we are./No, we aren't.
Are they pirates? Yes, they are./No, they aren't.

2 **Listen and circle.**

1 Yes, you are./
No, you aren't.

2 Yes, they are./
No, they aren't.

3 Yes, you are./
No, you aren't.

4 Yes, we are./
No, we aren't.

3 **Write** Yes, they are **or** No, they aren't.

1 Are they clowns?

Yes, they are.

2 Are they queens?

....

3 Are they pirates?

....

4 Are they cowboys?

....

5 Are they dancers?

....

4 **Play the game.**

Are you a clown?

No, I'm not.

Are you a king?

Yes, I am.

The grey duck

duck

happy

1

Hello. I'm your mum.

Hello, Mum.

Hello, I'm your dad.

Hello, Dad.

2

One, two, three, four, five yellow ducks! I'm happy.

Look! A grey duck.

3

Hello, are you my mum?

No, I'm not.

Is he my dad?

No, he isn't.

4

Is she my sister?

No, she isn't. She's a yellow duck. You are grey.

(1) Circle.

1 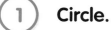 Is she a duck?
Yes, she is. / No, she isn't.

2 Is he small?
Yes, he is. / No, he isn't.

3  Is she yellow?
Yes, she is. / No, she isn't.

4  Are they swans?
Yes, they are. / No, they aren't.

small

big

sad

swan

5

Is he my brother?

No, he isn't. He's small and you're big.

6 The grey duck is sad.

Goodbye!

Bye, bye.

7

Hello, my baby. I'm your mum.

Am I a swan?

Yes, you are! We're swans.

8

I love you.

I love you, Mum.

They are a happy family.

---

2 Write with Karla.

This is my friend, Patty.
She's a girl.
She's seven.

This is my friend, ...

....

....

....

....

1 **Listen and circle.**

My family

1 ~~brother~~ dad   **2** sister mum

3 mum grandma   **4** dad grandpa

5 brother grandpa   **6** sister grandma

Now circle and write.

1 (He's)/ She's my ___brother___ .

2 He's / She's my _____ .

3 He's / She's my _____ .

4 He's / She's my _____ .

5 He's / She's my _____ .

6 He's / She's my _____ .

2 **Write** is/isn't **or** are/aren't.

1 He ___is___ a pirate.

2 He _____ small.

3 He _____ happy.

4 They _____ queens.

5 They _____ big.

6 They _____ sad.

3 Ask and answer.

1
2
3

4
5
6

Are they cowboys?

Are they clowns?

Are they number four?

No, they aren't.

Yes, they are.

Yes.

4 What about you? Write I am or I'm not.

1 .... a baby.
2 .... a boy.
3 .... a dancer.

4 .... a spy.
5 .... happy.

My Project

Draw a family tree.

This is my family.

My grandma Mo

My grandpa Fred

My dad Murphy

My mum Bronze

My grandma Goldie

My grandpa Silver

My brother Chimp

Chatter (me)

My sister Zee

Now go to

My Picture Dictionary

FUN TIME 1

1 **Say it with Sally.**

a) **Listen and point. Then repeat.**

p   b

t   d

b) **Listen and write. Then repeat.**

1  ..p.. encil

2 ....ag

3 ....iger

4 ....oll

5 ....eacher

6 ....uck

7 ....all

8 ....en

c) **Chant.**

Pens and pencils.   Books and bags.   Ducks and dogs.   Ten tigers.

2 **Look and write. Find the secret word.**

1 The queen is my m u m .
2 The king is my g _____ [p] ____ .
3 The clown is my ____ [   ] s _____ .
4 The dancer is my ____ [   ] ____ n _____ .
5 The spy is my ____ [   ] d .
6 The cowboy is my _____ o [   ] _____ .
7 The duck is my f _____ [   ] _____ .

I'm a p ____ .
2 3 4 5 6 7

3 **Find ten more differences. Then point and say.**

9

 kite   cloudy   computer game   old   radio   new   bike

It's his kite.

It's cloudy.

What a mess! What's this?

It's his kite. ... Oh, look! My computer game.

What's that?

It's her old doll.

Is that your box?

It isn't a box. It's her radio.

This is my new bike!

Be careful, Tag!

Come back, Chatter!

1 **Circle.**

1 It is / isn't my bike.

2 It is / isn't my computer game.

3 It is / isn't my kite.

4 It is / isn't my radio.

I'm Tag. This is my bike.

Learn with Tag

I am Tag.	My bike is new.
You are a tiger.	Your bike is grey.
He is a boy.	His kite is yellow.
She is a girl.	Her doll is old.
It is a doll.	Its clothes are pink.

2 **Choose and write.**

~~My~~   your   his   Her   its   my

1 ...My... name is Beth and I'm seven.
2 He's a king and this is .... crown.
3 She's my grandma. .... bag is blue.

4 It's a big dog. What's .... name?
5 You're happy. Is it .... birthday?
6 I'm Tessa and this is .... brother.

3 **Listen and stick. Then circle.**

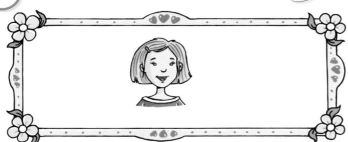

1 (His)/ Her bike is blue.
2 His / Her ball is orange.
3 His / Her radio is red.

4 His / Her car is green.
5 His / Her book is yellow.
6 His / Her kite is purple.

4 **Sing along with the FlyHigh band!**

What a terrible mess!

What's this? What's that?
What's this? What's that?
What's this? What's that?
What a terrible mess!

This is her radio.
This is her radio.
This is her radio.
Her radio is blue.

What's this? What's that?
What's this? What's that?
What's this? What's that?
What a terrible mess!

That is his bike.
That is his bike.
That is his bike.
His bike is new.

10

 toys rollerblades train slow fast winner prize

They're our toys.

1. Look at my toys.

They're our toys, Chatter.

2. What are they?

They're my rollerblades.

3. Here are Patty and Trumpet. Wow! Look at their train.

They're slow. I'm fast.

Let's race!

4. We are the winners!

Here are your prizes.

Thank you, Sally!

---

1) **Circle.**

1 It's his bike.
(yes) / no

2 It's her train.
yes / no

3 They're his rollerblades.
yes / no

4  They're the winners.
yes / no

You are the winners.
Your prizes are here.

We are brothers and sisters.
Our family is big.

They are slow.
Their bikes are old.

Learn with Tag

2 **Circle.**

1 They are happy. It's (their) / her birthday.
2 We are sisters and this is his / our mum.
3 You are friends. Is that my / your school?
4 They are brothers and that's its / their dad.

3 **Write** our, your **or** their.

1 They're ...our... presents.

2 It's .... ball.

3 It's .... dog.

4 It's .... car.

4 **Write with Karla.**

Here are my toys.
This is my computer game. This is my ball.
My favourite toy is my doll.

Here are ....
This is ....
This is ....
My favourite ....

leg	body	head	wing	hand	arm	feet

I've got a pet.

① I've got a pet. It's an insect. It's got six legs, a blue body, a small head and beautiful wings.

② She's got a pet. She's lucky.

INSECTS

Let's look at the insects.

③ They've got lots of legs.

Look. That's big.

④ They're on my hands and arms!

They're on my feet!

Oh, dear!

1 **Choose and write.**

beautiful   small      pet   ~~blue~~

1 Its body is ....blue........ .

2 Its head is ....

3 Its wings are ....

4 It's her ....

Learn with Tag

I've got an orange and black body.

I/You/We/They have got two legs. →
I/You/We/They've got two legs.

He/She/It has got small hands. →
He/She/It's got small hands.

2 **Choose and write.**

head   feet   wings   ~~legs~~   body

1 It's got six ....legs........... and ....
2 It's got a yellow and black ....
3 It's got a small black ....
4 It's got four ....

3 **Circle.**

1 I (have got) / has got a radio.
2 She have got / has got a watch.
3 You 've got / 's got a bag.

4 They have got / has got an umbrella.
5 It 've got / 's got a box.
6 The clown have got / has got a car.

4 **Sing along with the FlyHigh band!** ♫

We've got hands and feet.
We are boys and we are girls.
We've got hands and we've got feet.
We've got arms and we've got legs.
Let's all dance now to the beat.

Clap your hands and turn around.
Stamp your feet and touch the ground.
Clap your hands and turn around.
Stamp your feet and then sit down.

12

 ear

 mouth

 nose

 eye

 butterfly

 hair

 hair slide

Have we got all the insects?

① They're everywhere. Quick!
My ears.
My mouth.
My nose. Atishoo!

② Have we got all the insects?
No, we haven't. Look.
Wow! It's got beautiful eyes. Has it got wings?
Yes, it has.

③ It's a present for you, Chatter.
Thank you! Now I've got a pet.
Oh, look! You've got a butterfly in your hair, Sally.

④ No, I haven't. Look. It's a hair slide!

① **Match.**

1 The insects are
2 Sally has got a present for
3 Chatter has got
4 His insect has got
5 Sally has got a

a Chatter.
b everywhere.
c hair slide.
d a pet.
e wings.

Have you got a black nose?

Yes, I have.

Have I/you/we/they got brown eyes?

Has he/she/it got big ears?

Learn with Tag

Yes, I/you/we/they have.
No, I/you/we/they haven't.

Yes, he/she/it has.
No, he/she/it hasn't.

2 **Listen and circle.**

1 a    b

2 a    b

3 a    b

3 **Write** Yes, they have **or** No, they haven't.

1 Have elephants got big ears? ....Yes, they have.......
2 Have snakes got legs? ....
3 Have swans got wings? ....
4 Have zebras got arms? ....
5 Have whales got hair? ....

4 **Play the game.**

Has it got four legs?

Has it got wings?

Is it a butterfly?

No, it hasn't.

Yes, it has.

Yes, it is.

Sally's Story

Circus boy!

circus

funny

long

The clowns are very funny. Look at their arms and legs. They've got long arms and legs. I've got short arms and legs. I'm not funny.

The dancers are very beautiful. Look at their feet and hands. They've got beautiful feet and hands.

The monkeys are very fast. I'm not fast.

---

1 **Choose and write.**

star   fast   ~~funny~~   strong   beautiful

1 The clowns are ____funny____ .

2 The dancers are _____ .

3 The monkeys are _____ .

4 The elephants are _____ .

5 The boy is a _____ .

short strong trunk star

The elephants are strong. Look at their big trunks. I'm not very strong.

A small boy! Have we got a small boy in the circus?

Yes, we have!

Hooray! You're a star!

2 **Write with Karla.**

This is my friend, Sally.
She's got long hair.
She's got blue eyes.
She's got a small nose and a pink mouth.
She's happy.

This is my friend, ...
She's got ....
She's got ....
She's got ....
....
She's ....

1 Choose and write.

~~my~~   your   His   her   Our   their

1 I've got long arms and ....*my*.... hands are big.
2 We haven't got a new car. .... car is old.
3 He's got a new bike. .... bike is fast.
4 She's pretty and .... hair is long.
5 Elephants are grey and .... ears are big.
6 You are short and .... feet are small.

2 Listen and match.

1   **2**    **3**   **4**

a   **b**    **c**   **d**

3 Write have got/has got or haven't got/hasn't got.

1 He ....*has got*........ a car.
He ....*hasn't got*........ a train.

2 It .... an apple.
It .... a ball.

3 She .... a radio.
She .... a computer game.

4 They .... bikes.
They .... rollerblades.

4 Look and say.

He's got short hair. He's got brown eyes. He's got a big mouth.

It's number two.

1

2

3

4

5

6

5 What about you? Write Yes, I have or No, I haven't.

1 Have you got long ears? ....
2 Have you got short hair? ....
3 Have you got a small mouth? ....
4 Have you got blue eyes? ....
5 Have you got big feet? ....

My Project Draw and write about yourself.

My name's Maria. I'm a girl. I've got black hair and green eyes.

My name's Thomas. I'm a boy. I've got brown hair and blue eyes.

Now go to

My Picture Dictionary

13

 house swimming pool park river tree playground children

There's a town.

It's fantastic here. Look. There's a town.

Look at that big house and swimming pool.

There's a park and a river. The trees and flowers are very pretty.

Look at the playground!

There are lots of children here today.

Chatter's with the children.

Let's go to the playground.

1) **Find and number.**

the town 1   the park ....   the playground ....

the river ....   the swimming pool ....   the children ....

Learn with Tag

There is a tiger in the zoo. →
There's a tiger in the zoo.

There are lots of animals too.

2 **Find the differences and write.**

A

B

A
1 There are three ducks.
2 ....
3 ....

B
1 There are three swans.
2 ....
3 ....

3 **Listen and stick. Then write.**

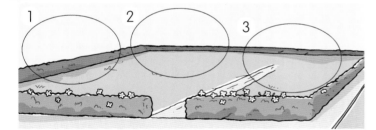

1 There are .... two trees ....
2 There's a ....
3 There's a ....

4 **Sing along with the FlyHigh band!** ♫

Animals in our zoo

There are lots of animals in our zoo.
Lions, tigers and kangaroos.
Bears and monkeys and zebras too.
We love the animals and they love you.

There are lots of animals in our zoo.
Snakes, penguins and cockatoos.
Goats and hippos and elephants too.
We love the animals and they love you.

14

 hot
 treehouse
 shop
 swing
 slide
 climbing frame
 bus

Where's Chatter?

It's hot. The animals are in the playground.

Where's Chatter?

I don't know. He isn't in the treehouse and he isn't in the shop.

He isn't on the swing.

He isn't on the slide.

He isn't under the climbing frame.

Look. There's Chatter. He's next to the bus.

Sorry, Sally. Goodbye.

Chatter, come here, please.

Goodbye, Chatter.

1) **Circle.**

1	There's a yellow climbing frame.	yes / no
2	There's a red slide.	yes / no
3	There are two swings.	yes / no
4	There are two children.	yes / no
5	There's a green bus.	yes / no

Learn with Tag

Where is Tag? → Where's Tag?
Where are Tag and Chatter?

in   on   under   next to

(2) **Write** Where's **or** Where are.

1 ....Where's................. Tag?
2 .... Chatter and Karla?
3 .... Sally?
4 .... Patty and Trumpet?

(3) **Choose and write.**

in   on   under   next to

1 The children are ....on.......... the climbing frame.
2 The ball is .... the slide.
3 The girl is .... the swing.
4 The cats are .... the treehouse.
5 The dog is .... the climbing frame.

(4) **Write with Karla.**

In our town, there's a park.
There's a swimming pool.
There are lots of shops.
There isn't a circus.

In my town, there's a ....
There's ....
There are ....
There isn't ....

 sing
 jump
 high
 ride
 swim
 climb
 play the guitar

I can sing.

① Wow! Look at Karla. She can jump very high!

② Be careful, Tag! He can ride his bike very fast.

③ Patty can swim. She's fantastic!

④ Chatter can climb trees!

Look at me. I can sing. I can play the guitar, listen!

No, that's terrible!

It's OK, Chatter.

1 **Match.**

1 Karla

2 Tag

3 Patty

4 Chatter

She's fantastic.

It's very high.

It's terrible.

He's very fast.

Learn with Tag

I **can** ride my bike very fast!

I/You/He/She/It/We/They **can** jump.

(2) **Choose and write.**

swim   climb a tree   play the guitar   ~~jump very high~~

1 I .... can jump very high ....

2 They ....

3 She ....

4 He ....

(3) **Sing along with the FlyHigh band!** ♫

I can

Look, look, look at me.
I can climb a tree.
I can read and I can write.
I can ride a bike.
Look, look, look at me.
I can swim in the sea.
I can jump up very high.
I can touch the sky.
Look, look, look at me.
I can count to three.
I can clap and turn around.
I can touch the ground.

16

 skip
 rollerblade
 fly
 do a handstand
 walk
 run
 carry

Can you skip?

① Come and play, Trumpet. Can you rollerblade?

No, I can't.

② Can you fly a kite?

No, I can't. I can't skip. I can't do a handstand.

③ They can do lots of things. I can't.

Yes, you can. You can walk and run.

④ You can carry everyone. We can't carry you!

---

1 **Choose and write.**

skip   carry everyone   do a handstand   ~~rollerblade~~   fly a kite

1 Chatter can _____rollerblade_____ .

2 Karla can _____ .

3 Tag can _____ .

4 Patty can _____ .

5 Trumpet can _____ .

I can't fly.

Learn with Tag

Can I/you/he/she/it/we/they fly?

Yes, I/you/he/she/it/we/they can.
No, I/you/he/she/it/we/they can't.

Can he skip? Yes, he can.

2 **Listen and draw 😊 or ☹.**

😊 = she can　　☹ = she can't

3 **Play the game.**

	run	climb trees	fly	jump

Can they climb trees?

Can they run?

Snakes.

Yes, they can.

No, they can't.

Sally's Story
Where's my mobile phone?

mobile phone

desk

cupboard

① Kelly and her mum are in the living room.

What's the matter, Mum?

I can't find my mobile phone.

② There are pens and pencils and crayons on the desk, but my mobile phone isn't here.

Is it on the desk?

③ Is it in the cupboard, Kelly?

No, it isn't.

④ It isn't under the computer.

---

(1) Read and answer.

1 Who can't find her phone? .... *Mum.*
2 Are the pens and pencils on the table? ....
3 Where are the books? ....
4 Is the mobile phone under the table? ....
5 What's the phone number? ....
6 Who's got the phone? ....

computer

bookcase

table

bed

5 Is it in the bookcase?

No, it isn't. There are lots of books in the bookcase, but your phone isn't here.

7 I've got an idea. What's your number?

It's 678945213.

6 It isn't on the table.

It isn't under the table.

8 Look, Mum! Fred's got the phone! It's in his bed!

Thank you, Kelly!

---

2 **Write with Karla.**

I can skip and fly a kite.
I can't play the guitar.
My friend can ride a bike.
My friend can't skip.

I can ....

I can't ....

My friend can ....

My friend can't ....

The FlyHigh Review (4)

1 **Choose and write.**

~~swimming pool~~ slide trees cupboard flowers swing bed school

1 In the town, there's a ....swimming pool........ and a ....
2 In the park, there are .... and ....
3 In the playground, there's a .... and a ....
4 In the bedroom, there's a .... and a ....

2 **Choose and write.**

in   on   under   next to   desk   cupboard   bed   table

1 Where's the computer?   ....It's on the desk..........
2 Where's the bookcase?   ....
3 Where's the bus?   ....
4 Where's the doll?   ....
5 Where are the clothes?   ....

3 **Listen and circle.**

1 (Yes, there is.) / No, there isn't.
2 Yes, there is. / No, there isn't.
3 Yes, there are. / No, there aren't.
4 Yes, there is. / No, there isn't.
5 Yes, there are. / No, there aren't.

4 Look and say.

"He can fly a kite."

"It's number two."

5 What about you? Write.

1 Can you sing?

2 Can you do a handstand?

3 Can you ride a bike?

4 Can your mum swim?

5 Can your dad play the guitar?

My Project

Draw three friends in a playground. Write about your friends.

Anna is on the swing.
Sam is next to the climbing frame.
Bill is in the tree house.

Now go to
My Picture Dictionary

17

 breakfast hungry bread honey milk egg orange

I like breakfast.

1 Circle.

1 Trumpet is small / hungry

2 There are eggs / cakes for breakfast.

3 There are bananas / oranges for breakfast.

4 Chatter, Patty and Karla have / haven't got their breakfast.

5 Trumpet is very naughty / good.

I like bananas.
I don't like oranges.

I like/don't like bananas.
You like/don't like bananas.
We like/don't like bananas.
They like/don't like bananas.

2 **Write.**

1. I .... like eggs ....

2. We ....

3. They ....

4. You ....

3 **Listen and stick.**

4 **Sing along with the FlyHigh band!**

I like breakfast.

I like milk and I like bread.
I like honey and I like eggs.
I like apples and oranges too.
I like breakfast.
How about you?

I like breakfast in the morning.
I like breakfast in the morning.
I like breakfast in the morning.
I like breakfast.
How about you?

18

 fish   lunch   pizza   soup   chicken   salad

Do you like fish, Patty?

1 It's time for lunch.
Do you like pizza, Karla?
Yes, I do.

2 Do you like soup, Patty?
No, I don't.

3 Do you like chicken, Patty? Do you like salad?
No, I don't.

4 Do you like fish, Patty?
Yes, I do!

5 Do you like me, Patty?
Yes, I do!

---

(1) **Circle.**

1	It's time for breakfast.	yes / (no)
2	Tag's got pizza.	yes / no
3	Sally's got a bowl of soup.	yes / no
4	Patty likes fish.	yes / no
5	Patty and Trumpet are friends.	yes / no

Learn with Tag

Do you like honey? Yes, I do.
Do you like oranges? No, I don't.

2 **Write.**

1 Do you like chicken? 😊 Yes, I do.   **3** Do you like soup? ☹ ....
2 Do you like pizza? 😊 ....   **4** Do you like salad? 😊 ....

3 **Write. Then answer about you.**

1  Do you like chicken? ....

2 ....

3 ....

4 **Play the game.**

Chicken and salad, please!

Soup, salad and eggs, please!

Chicken, soup, salad and eggs.

5 **Write with Karla.**

I like chicken and salad.
I don't like soup.

I like ....
....

I don't like ....
....

 get up

 seven o'clock

 have breakfast

 clean my teeth

 go to school

He gets up at seven o'clock.

① What do you do every day, Rob?

② I get up at seven o'clock, I have breakfast and I clean my teeth. I go to school at eight o'clock.

③ He gets up at seven o'clock, he has breakfast and he cleans his teeth. He goes to school at eight o'clock every day.

④ What's the time?

It's eight o'clock.

Let's go to his school!

Yes!

1 **Number in order.**

1

Learn with Tag

He clean**s** his teeth every day.
She get**s** up at seven o'clock every day.
It drink**s** milk every day.

2 **Write and circle.**

a  b  c  d

1 ....She gets up.......... at five o'clock / (seven o'clock.)
2 .... at nine o'clock / eight o'clock.
3 .... at four o'clock / six o'clock.
4 .... at eight o'clock / nine o'clock.

3 **Sing along with** the **FlyHigh** band! ♫

We all love our zoo.

Every day at three o'clock,
I come to the zoo.
I see my friends and we all play,
In my favourite zoo.

Chatter and Trumpet,
Karla and Tag,
Patty and Sally too.
They love me and I love them.
We all love our zoo.

Every day at three o'clock,
He goes to the zoo.
He sees his friends and they all play,
In his favourite zoo.

Chatter and Trumpet,
Karla and Tag,
Patty and Sally too.
They love him and he loves them.
They all love,
We all love our zoo!

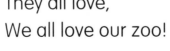

Monday Tuesday Wednesday Thursday Friday Saturday Sunday

Does Rob go to the zoo every day?

1 **Circle.**

1 The animals go to the zoo.   yes / no
2 Mr Light is a teacher.   yes / no
3 Rob goes to school every day.   yes / no
4 Rob goes to the zoo every day.   yes / no
5 The children love the zoo.   yes / no

Learn with Tag

Does he go to school every day? No, he doesn't.
Does he play basketball every day? Yes, he does.

2 **Listen and circle. Then answer.**

| Monday | Thursday |

| Tuesday | Friday |

| Wednesday  |

1 Does Rob ride his bike on Monday?   Yes, he does.
2 Does Rob swim on Tuesday?   ....
3 Does Rob play the guitar on Wednesday?   ....
4 Does Rob play basketball on Thursday?   ....
5 Does Rob go to the park on Friday?   ....

3 **Play the game.**

Look at me. What day is it?

Is it Friday?

Yes, it is!

Superboy

help

people

police officer

Superboy helps people every day of the week.

I'm Superboy! I am very strong. I can fly!

On Monday he helps old people.

Thank you, Superboy!

It's my pleasure.

On Tuesday he helps children.

Thank you, Superboy!

Have a good day, children!

On Wednesday he helps police officers.

Well done, Superboy!

Don't mention it!

---

1 **Choose and write.**

firemen   children   ~~old people~~   police officers   animals

1 On Monday, he helps .... old people ....

2 On Tuesday, he helps ....

3 On Wednesday, he helps ....

4 On Thursday, he helps ....

5 On Friday, he helps ....

fireman

visit

do my homework

On Thursday he helps firemen.

5

You're very strong, Superboy!

Yes, I am.

On Friday he helps animals.

6

You're very good, Superboy.

I know.

On Saturday he visits his grandma and grandpa.

7

Help yourself, Superboy.

Thank you, Grandma!

But on Sunday he does his homework.
Help Superboy with his homework!

8

Ten and two is ...

---

2 **Write with Karla.**

MONDAY
MAY
5

Monday	I clean my teeth. I go to school.
Tuesday	
Wednesday	
Thursday	
Friday	
Saturday	
Sunday	

1 Write.

1 bread

2

3

4

5

6

7

8

9

2 What about you? Write Yes, I do or No, I don't.

1 Do you like milk?

2 Do you like chicken?

3 Do you like fish soup?

4 Do you like apples and oranges?

5 Do you like bread and honey?

3 Ask your friend.

	yes	no

1 Do you get up at seven o'clock?

2 Do you go to school at eight o'clock?

3 Do you play basketball every day?

4 Do you do your homework at six o'clock?

Now write Yes, he/she does **or** No, he/she doesn't.

1 Does your friend get up at seven o'clock?

2 Does your friend go to school at eight o'clock?

3 Does your friend play basketball every day?

4 Does your friend do homework at six o'clock?

4 Listen and circle. Then match.

1 a  b

2 a  b

3 a  b

4 a  b

1 Polly Pink gets up at
2 She has
3 She goes to dancing school at
4 She goes to bed at

a eleven o'clock.
b ten o'clock.
c an orange and a banana for breakfast.
d nine o'clock.

My Project

Make a class food chart. Then write.

	🍎	🥚	🥛	🍗
Anna	☺	☹	☺	☺
Ben	☺	☺	☹	☺
David	☹	☺	☺	☺
Sarah	☺	☺	☺	☹
Mary	☺	☺	☹	☺
Peter	☺	☺	☺	☹

Five pupils like apples. One pupil doesn't like apples.

Now go to

My Picture Dictionary

FUN TIME 2

1 Say it with Sally.

a) Listen and point. Then repeat.

a **e**

U **i**

o

b) Listen and write. Then repeat.

1 i̲nsect   2 ......range   3 ......mbrella

4 ......gg   5 ......pple   6 fr......g

7 d......ck   8 c......t   9 n......st

10 h......ppo

c) Chant.

Black cats.   Eggs in a nest.   Pink insects.   Orange frogs.   Mum and an umbrella.

2 Draw and write. Then ask and answer.

1 odiar
radio

2 tkei

3 cmueoptr

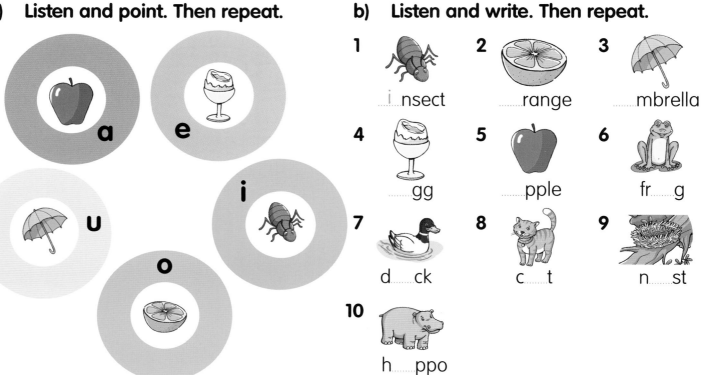

Where's the radio?

4 rtuaig

5 sub

6 sbrleraldleo

It's on the table.

21

 play read sleep hide water pistol come

I'm playing a game!

① Sally, I'm doing my homework! I'm reading.

I'm writing.

Very good!

② Look at Chatter. He's sleeping.

③ Ssh!

Oh, you're hiding!

Yes! I'm playing a game.

④ Tag has got a big water pistol! Run! He's coming!

1 **Circle.**

1 Patty has got a phone / (pencil.)
2 Trumpet has got a book / pen.
3 Tag has got a kite / water pistol.
4 The water pistol is small / big.

I'm hiding.

Learn with Tag

I am hiding. → I'm hiding.
You are writing. → You're writing.
He is playing. → He's playing.
She is reading. → She's reading.
It is sleeping. → It's sleeping.

2 **Circle and write.**

1 He /(She) .... is reading ....

2 He / She ....

3 He / She ....

4 He / She ....

3 **Listen and stick. Then write.**

1 I'm .... reading ....

2 He's ....

3 She's ....

4 **Sing along with the FlyHigh band!**

I'm playing.

I'm playing with my friends.
I'm playing with my friends.
Hey ho, away we go.
I'm playing with my friends.

She's hiding from her friends.
She's hiding from her friends.
Hey ho, away we go.
She's hiding from her friends.

22

 have a shower
 trousers
 T-shirt
 shoes
 skirt
 dress
 sweater

They're having a shower.

Look at my trousers and T-shirt and shoes!

Look at my skirt!

You're wearing a pretty dress and sweater, Sally.

Thank you.

Where are Chatter, Trumpet and Tag?

They're playing in the river.

We're coming!

Oh! They're having a shower!

---

1 **Circle.**

1 Sally is wearing a skirt.   yes / no
2 Patty is wearing a T-shirt.   yes / no
3 Chatter is playing in the river.   yes / no
4 Tag is having a shower.   yes / no

You're wearing trousers.

Learn with Tag

We are wearing trousers. → We're wearing trousers.
You are wearing trousers. → You're wearing trousers.
They are wearing trousers. → They're wearing trousers.

2 **Circle and write.**

1 (We're) / They're
wearing pink
dresses.

2 We're / They're
....
trousers.

3 We're / They're
....
T-shirts.

3 **Write.**

blue
trousers

4 **Write with Karla.**

I'm wearing a green sweater, yellow trousers and red shoes.
My friend is wearing a white T-shirt, a blue skirt and
black shoes.

I'm wearing ....
....
My friend ....
....

23

basketball volleyball football tennis idea tired

They aren't swimming!

1 Tag is playing basketball. I'm not playing basketball.

2 Karla and Trumpet are playing volleyball. I'm not playing volleyball.

3 I'm not playing football. I'm not playing tennis.

I've got a good idea!

4 You're swimming, Patty! They aren't swimming!

I'm tired.

1 **Choose and write.**

volleyball   tennis   swimming   football   ~~basketball~~

1 Tag is playing ....basketball........ .

2 Karla and Trumpet are playing ....

3 Chatter is playing ....

4 Rob is playing ....

5 Patty is ....

Learn with Tag

I am not play**ing**. → I'm not play**ing**.

He/She/It is not play**ing**. →
He/She/It isn't play**ing**.

We/You/They are not play**ing**. →
We/You/They aren't play**ing**.

2 **Find the differences and write.**

A

B

1 The boys are playing basketball.
2 ....
3 ....
4 ....

1 The boys aren't playing basketball.
2 ....
3 ....
4 ....

3 **Sing along with the FlyHigh band!** ♫

Splish and splash
I'm not playing basketball.
I'm not playing volleyball.
I'm not playing football.
I'm not playing tennis.

I'm swimming in the sea today.
I'm splashing in the sea today.
Splish and splash,
Splish and splash,
I'm swimming in the sea today.

24

 dream

 noise

 eat

 drink

 upstairs

 roar

 snore

Are they sleeping? 🎵

Are they sleeping? Are they dreaming?
Where are the animals?
What are they doing?
Are they reading? Are they writing?
What is that terrible noise?

Are you eating? Are you drinking?
Where are you, animals?
What are you doing?
Are you playing? Are you hiding?
What is that terrible noise?

② Hide all the toys! Eat all the cake!
Jump into bed! Sally is coming upstairs!

③ We're not playing.
We're not eating.
Look at us, Sally,
We're very good animals.
Tag's not roaring.
Trumpet's snoring.
That is the terrible noise!

---

1 **Match.**

Picture one   ......e......

Picture two   .... , ...

Picture three .... , ... , ...

a The animals are very good.
b Tag is hiding the toys.
c Trumpet is eating.
d Trumpet's snoring.
e The animals are playing.
f The animals are sleeping.

Learn with Tag

Are you sleeping, Tag?

No, I'm not.

Am I sleeping?
Yes, you are./No, you aren't.

Is he/she/it sleeping?
Yes, he is./No, he isn't.

Are you/we/they sleeping?
Yes, we are./No, we aren't.

2 **Listen and circle. Then answer.**

1  yes / no

2  yes / no

3  yes / no

4  yes / no

5  yes / no

6  yes / no

No, she isn't.

1 Is Bella doing her homework?
2 Is she having a shower?
3 Is George reading?
4 Is he writing?
5 Is Dad sleeping?
6 Are Bella, George and Dad playing on the computer?

3 **Play the game.**

Are you writing 'ball'?

No, I'm not.

Are you writing 'baby'?

Yes, I am.

Sally's Story

Jane and the giant

giant

hear

Jane can see a big house. It has got lots of doors and windows. She can hear a noise.

1 Hey, ho, hi, humming. I'm a giant. I am coming!

Jane is in the living room. She is hiding under a table. She can hear the giant.

2 Micky, mocky, mucky, mig! I'm a giant. I am big.

Jane is in the bathroom now. She is hiding in the shower. She can hear the giant.

3 Flippy, floppy, flappy, flong! I'm a giant. I am strong.

Jane is in the kitchen. She is hiding in the cupboard. She can hear the giant.

4 Wiz, woz, woodle, weet! I'm a giant. I've got big feet.

(1) **Choose and write.**

kitchen   living room   ~~bedroom~~   bathroom

1 Jane is hiding in the bed here. ......bedroom......

2 Jane is hiding in the cupboard here. ....

3 Jane is hiding under the table here. ....

4 Jane is hiding in the shower here. ....

living room   bathroom   kitchen   bedroom   ghost

Jane is in the bedroom now. She is hiding in the bed. She can hear the giant.

5

Bing, bang, bong, begs! I'm a giant. I've got long legs.

6

He's got a big head, long arms and big feet!

I can hear a girl!

Jane has got a good idea. She is standing on the bed.

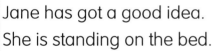

7

Apples, jelly, cakes and toast! Look at me. I'm a ghost!

8

Goodnight, giant. Sweet dreams!

2 **Write with Karla.**

bedroom

This is our home. We've got two bedrooms.

The FlyHigh Review 6

1 Circle and write.

1  I (am) / are ......reading...... .

2  She am / is ....

3  It is / are ....

4 He is / are ....

5  You is / are ....

2 Match.

1 I am doing
2 You are doing
3 We are doing
4 They are doing

a their homework.
b our homework.
c my homework.
d your homework.

3 Write.

1 ......T-shirt......

2 ....

3 ....

4 ....

5  ....

6  ....

4 Write.

1

2

1 The girl is wearing an orange T-shirt .
She is ....
She ....

2 The boy is wearing ....
He ....
He ....

5 **Listen and circle. Then answer.**

The giant is in the (kitchen) / bedroom. He is playing / doing his homework. His mum is snoring / writing. His dad is playing football / tennis in the living room / kitchen. His brother and sister are having a shower / hiding in the shower.

1 Is the giant in the kitchen?   Yes, he is.
2 Is the giant doing his homework?
3 Is his mum writing?
4 Is his dad playing tennis?
5 Are his brother and sister having a shower?

6 **What about you? Write.**

1 Are you writing?
2 Are you standing up?
3 Are you wearing trousers?
4 What are you doing?

My Project

Draw a house. Describe it.

The house is big and yellow. The door is red and the windows are green. There is a bathroom, a bedroom, a kitchen and a living room.

Now go to

My Picture Dictionary

25

 crab

 raining

 dolphin

 turtle

 camera

 take a photo

These are crabs.

1 **Circle.**

1 It's raining / sunny.
2 Patty and Tag are eating / looking at the fish.
3 The dolphin is swimming / reading in the pool.
4 Patty has got her watch / camera.
5 There's a turtle / crab in the photo.

Learn with Tag

This is **an octopus.**
These are **crabs.**

2 **Write** This is **or** These are.

1 .... This is .... my watch.
2 .... your trousers.
3 .... his shoes.
4 .... her dress.
5 .... your T-shirt.
6 .... our clothes.

3 **Listen and stick. Then match.**

a These are fish. **b** This is a dolphin. **c** These are crabs. **d** This is a turtle.

4 **Sing along with the FlyHigh band!** ♫

This is a fish.

This is a fish.
It's swimming in the sea.
I can see the fish
And it can see me.
It can see me.

These are dolphins.
They're swimming in the sea.
I can see the dolphins
And they can see me.
They can see me.

men   feed   women   tall   shark   teeth

There are lots of people.

1 There are lots of people next to the pool. Two men are feeding the fish.

I can't see. These women are very tall.

Come here, Patty!

2

Wow! Look at this shark! Look at its teeth! Patty, where are you?

3 I'm here.

Patty, there's a big shark in the pool.

It's OK. The shark is my friend!

1 **Match.**

1 Lots of people are next to the   **a** fish.
2 Two men are feeding the   **b** tall.
3 The women are very   **c** teeth.
4 Tag can see a   **d** pool.
5 The shark's got lots of   **e** shark.

Learn with Tag

+ es		ƴ + ies		Irregular plurals	
fox	foxes	baby	babies	child	children
bus	buses	family	families	man	men
dress	dresses	spy	spies	woman	women
watch	watches			foot	feet
				tooth	teeth

2 **Circle.**

1 The spy / (spies) have got a camera.
2 My dad's got big foot / feet.
3 This box / boxes is small.

4 Have you got a watch / watches?
5 She's got three dress / dresses.
6 There are two man / men in the pool.

3 **Choose and write.**

baby   fox   woman   ~~child~~   man

1 The ___children___ are on the swings.
2 The _____ are sleeping.
3 The _____ are reading.
4 The _____ are playing tennis.
5 The _____ are hiding.

4 **Write with Karla.**

Look at my photos.

This is a shark. Look at its teeth.

These are my friends.

This _____
_____ .

These _____
_____ .

27

 bowl
 carrot
 drawer
 shelf
 cherry
 sweets
 chocolate

There are some apples.

There are some apples in the bowl.
There are some carrots in the drawer.
There are some bananas on the shelf.
But we're looking for the **Secret Store**!

Are there any cherries?
Are there any sweets?
Are there any chocolates?
Are there any treats?

There aren't any cherries in the bowl.
There aren't any sweets in the drawer.
There aren't any chocolates on the shelf.
But here it is, the **Secret Store**!

There are lots of cherries.
There are lots of sweets.
There are lots of chocolates.
There are lots of treats.

1 Match.

1 The apples are   **a** on the shelf.
2 The carrots are   **b** in the bowl.
3 The bananas are   **c** in the box.
4 The cherries are   **d** in the drawer.

Learn with Tag

There are some bananas.
There aren't any cherries.
Are there any apples? Yes, there are.
Are there any carrots? No, there aren't.

2 **Write** some **or** any.

1 There are ....some........ cars in the toy box.
2 Are there .... dolls?
3 There aren't .... yo-yos.
4 There are .... balls.

3 **Write.**

1 apples   There are some apples.
2 sweets   There aren't any sweets.
3 bananas   ....
4 cherries   ....
5 carrots   ....
6 chocolates ....

4 **Ask and answer.**

Are there any chairs in your classroom?

Yes, there are.

chairs   rabbits
windows   pencils
cakes   water
fish   pistols
books   crayons
boys

28

11 eleven **12** twelve **13** thirteen **14** fourteen **15** fifteen **16** sixteen **17** seventeen

How many sweets are there?

(1) **Circle and count. Then write the number of sweets.** ....

18 19 20
eighteen   nineteen   twenty

What are they? They are sweets.
Where are they? They are in the box.
Who's got the sweets? Tag's got the sweets.
How many are there? There are five.

2 Listen and write.

1  20

2

3

4

5

6

3 Choose and write. Then answer.

What   Where   Who   How many

1 ....What.......... are you doing? ....
2 .... pens have you got? ....
3 .... is your bag? ....
4 .... are you wearing? ....
5 .... is your teacher? ....

4 Play the game.

How many pencils are there?

No.

Yes.

Eleven.

Five.

Sally's Story

Harry and Greta

 forest biscuit

Harry and his sister go for a walk in the forest. They see a beautiful house.

①

Look at that house, Greta.

There are sweets, cakes, bananas and cherries on the doors and windows. There are biscuits and chocolates on the walls.

②

A very old woman lives in the house. She has got a big nose and small black eyes.

③ Good morning. I've got some cakes and sweets in my house. Please come in. I've got some apples, bananas and lots of chocolate.

Thank you.

④ These cherries are for you, little boy and this big cake is for you, little girl.

---

① **Read and answer.**

1 Where is the house? .... *It is in the forest.* ....
2 What is on the walls? ....
3 Who's got the cherries? ....
4 Who's in the cupboard? ....
5 What can Greta see in the trees? ....
6 Is the old woman happy? ....

wall
 little
 squirrel
 angry

5 Aha! Now I've got you! Get in the cupboard!

Help!

The squirrels eat the biscuits, cakes and chocolates. They eat the walls and the doors! Greta opens the cupboard.

7

Stop it! You are eating my house!

Greta sees some squirrels in the trees.

6

Please, come and help my brother!

Greta and Harry run away. They are happy. The old woman is very angry.

8 Thank you, squirrels!

---

2 **Write with Karla.**

In our kitchen, there are some apples.
There are some bananas.
There aren't any biscuits.
There aren't any cakes.

In our kitchen, there are

....

There ....

There aren't ....

There ....

1 **Find the odd one out. Then write.**

1 apples (sharks) cherries bananas
2 crabs men women children
3 cakes biscuits chocolates dolphins
4 eleven fourteen turtles nineteen
5 fish teeth hair feet

You can see (**1**) _sharks_ , (**2**) _____ , (**3**) _____ ,
(**4**) _____ and (**5**) _____ in the sea.

2 **Write.**

1 (box) The _boxes_ are on the shelf.
2 (cherry) Where are the _____ ?
3 (tooth) How many _____ have you got?
4 (baby) The _____ are sleeping.
5 (bus) The school _____ are yellow.
6 (child) The _____ are in the playground.

3 **Listen and circle. Then write.**

1 (a) **b**

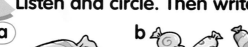

This is a sweet.

2 a **b**

These are biscuits.

3 a **b** **4 a** **b**

5 a **b** **6 a** **b**

4 Look and say.

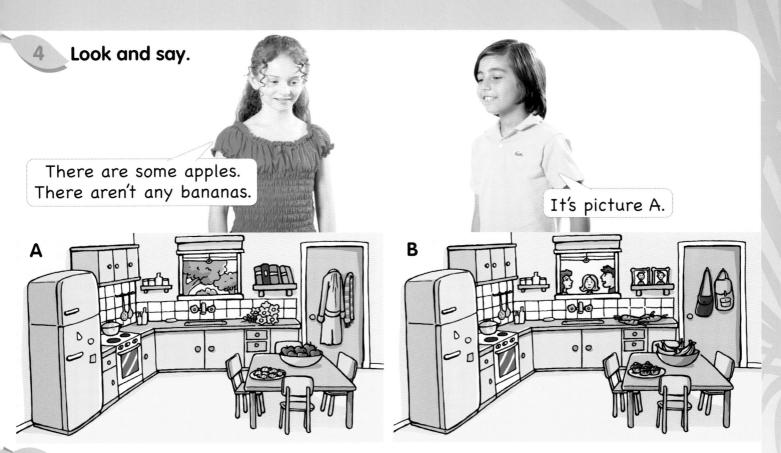

There are some apples.
There aren't any bananas.

It's picture A.

A

B

5 What about you? Write.

1 How many children are there in your class? ....
2 How many chairs are there in the classroom? ....
3 How many books are there in your bag? ....
4 How many letters are there in your name? ....

My Project

Make an underwater collage.

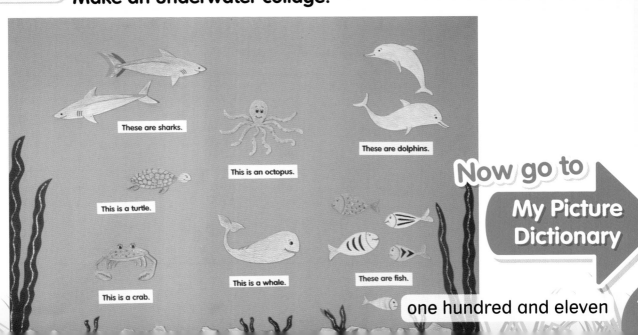

These are sharks.

This is an octopus.

These are dolphins.

This is a turtle.

This is a whale.

These are fish.

This is a crab.

Now go to

My Picture Dictionary

FUN TIME 3

1 Say it with Sally.

a) Listen and point. Then repeat.

f

v

w

h

b) Listen and write. Then repeat.

1 h.....ippo

2 .....ox

3 .....hale

4  .....ulture

5 .....lower

6 ri.....er

7 .....ouse

8 s.....an

c) Chant.

Happy hippos.   We're winners.   Visiting vultures.   Funny foxes.

2 Play bingo.

Draw and write a different food in each square.

....	....	....	....
....	....	....	....

3 Label the rooms. Then answer.

bedroom   bathroom   kitchen   living room

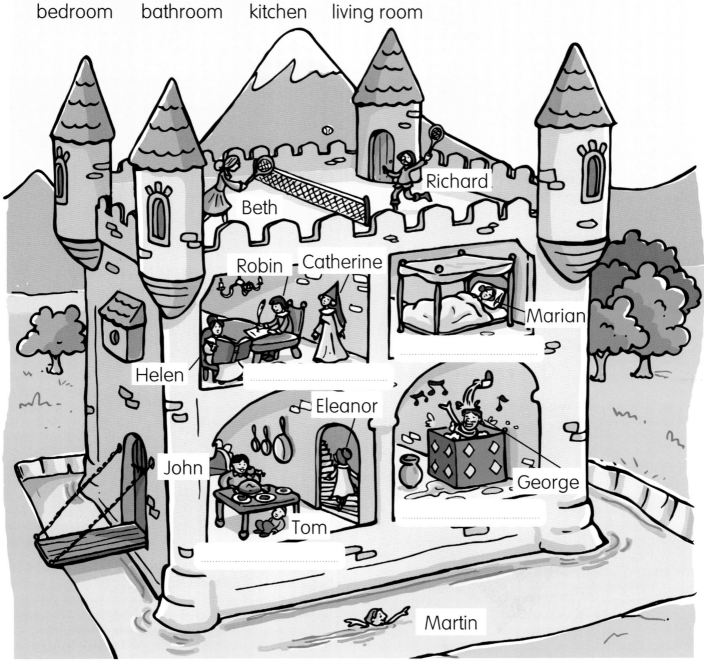

1 Who is singing? George
2 Who is playing tennis?
3 Who is swimming?
4 Who is sleeping?
5 Who is reading?
6 Who is eating?

7 Who is wearing a
   long dress?
8 Who is going upstairs?
9 Who is hiding?
10 Who is writing?

Now draw a ghost in one of the rooms. Your friends guess where it is.

Happy Christmas!

reindeer

Christmas tree

star

Father Christmas

1 It's Christmas.

Hello, reindeer. Are you ready? Let's go. Ho, ho, ho.

2

Look at the Christmas tree and the stars.

It's very pretty. Listen. What is it?

3

It's Father Christmas ...

... and the Christmas presents!

4 Look. It's a robot! What's your present?

It's a doll!

5 The children are very happy.

Thank you, Father Christmas!

1 **Count and write.**

[1] tree   [....] stars   [....] balls   [....] presents   [....] cards

2 **Sing along with the FlyHigh band!** ♫

Jingle bells

Jingle bells, jingle bells,
Jingle all the way.
Jingle bells, jingle bells,
Hurray, it's Christmas Day!

3 **Make a Christmas card.**

 throw   streamers   mask   dance   laugh

(1) Sing along with the FlyHigh band! ♫

I'm a cowboy, you're a dancer.
Happy Carnival to you!
We are clowns and they are pirates.
Happy Carnival to you!

Throw your streamers, put your masks on.
Happy Carnival to you!
Dance and laugh with all your friends now.
Happy Carnival to you!

(2) Make a mask.

Happy Easter!

Easter egg

paint

1
Hello. What's your name?

I'm Easter Bunny.

You've got lots of eggs!

They are for the children at Easter. I'm painting them.

2
What are you doing now?

I'm hiding the eggs in the flowers and trees.

3
Sit here. Look!

I've got a big orange egg!

I've got two small pink eggs!

4
Happy Easter, children!

Thank you, Easter Bunny!

Sing along with the FlyHigh band! ♫

Easter Bunny's in the garden.

Easter Bunny's in the garden, hiding eggs.
Easter Bunny's in the garden, hiding toys.
He is hiding eggs and toys in the flowers and the trees.
Easter Bunny's in the garden. Come with me.

The FlyHigh

Sally:	Hello! I'm Sally and I'm the keeper in our zoo!
All sing:	Welcome to our zoo!
Child 1:	There is a monkey, a tiger, a kangaroo, a penguin and an elephant in the zoo.
All sing:	Animals in our zoo (Lesson 13)
Trumpet:	I'm Trumpet. I'm an elephant. I like school.
Karla:	I'm Karla. I'm a kangaroo. At school we read and write and play.
Child 2:	Do you go to school every day?
Trumpet:	No. We go to school on Monday, Tuesday, Wednesday, Thursday and Friday.
Child 1:	Are you happy today?
All:	Yes, we are!
All sing:	We're happy today. (Lesson 7)

Music Show

Chatter: My name's Chatter. I'm a monkey. I can climb trees!

Patty: I'm Patty. I'm a penguin. I can swim in the sea.

Tag: My name's Tag. I'm a tiger. I can play basketball.

All sing: I can (Lesson 15)

Child 2: I'm hungry! Have we got any apples and oranges? I like apples and oranges!

All sing: I like breakfast. (Lesson 17)

Child 1: Sally, are the animals in the zoo good?

Sally: Yes, they are!

Children 1 & 2: We love the animals in the zoo!

All sing: We all love our zoo. (Lesson 19)

Sally: We love our families and friends! We love you!

All sing: My family (Lesson 5)

All: Goodbye!

My Picture Dictionary

Listen, point and say. Then write.

①
school

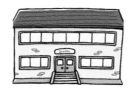
....

....

....

....

....

....

....

....

....

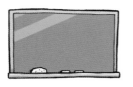
....

....

....

....

....

....

....

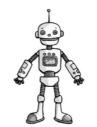
....

....

....

....

....

....

....

....

....

....

....

....

....

....

....

....

....

....

....

....

....

....

....

....

....

....

....

....

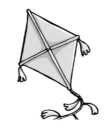

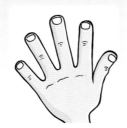

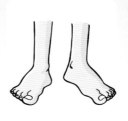

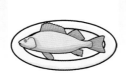

Pearson Education Limited
Edinburgh Gate
Harlow
Essex CM20 2JE
England
and Associated Companies throughout the world.

www.pearsonelt.com

First published 2010
Sixteenth impression 2018

ISBN: 978-1-4082-4630-6

Printed in Malaysia (CTP-VVP)

Set in VagRounded

llustrated by: GS Animation/Grupa Smacznego,
Christos Skaltsas/eyscream, Zaharias Papadopoulos/eyscream,
Katerina Chrysochoou
Digital illustrations by: HL Studios, Long Hanborough, Oxford

Acknowledgements
The publishers and authors would like to thank all the consultants,
schools and teachers who helped to develop this course for their
valuable feedback and comments.

Lesson 1

Lesson 4

Review 1

Lesson 5

Lesson 9

Lesson 13

Lesson 17

Lesson 21

Lesson 25